PETER SCHUMANN

ALL NOTHING NOTHING AT ALL

MAY 2020

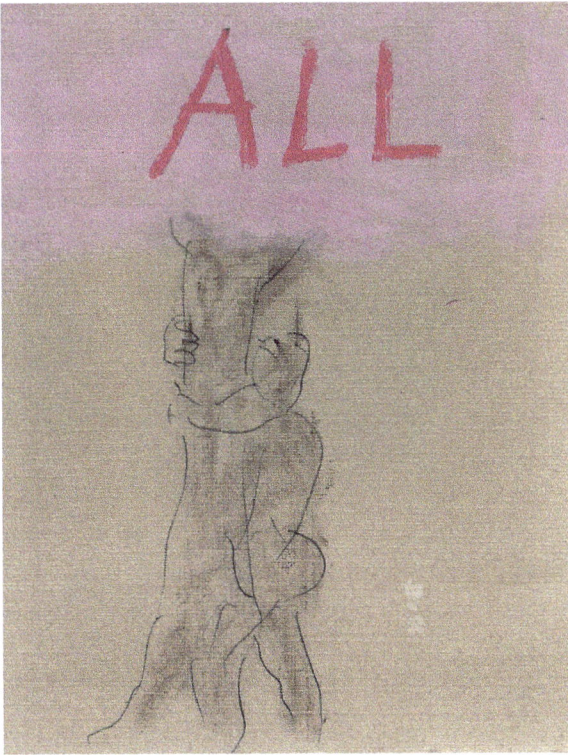

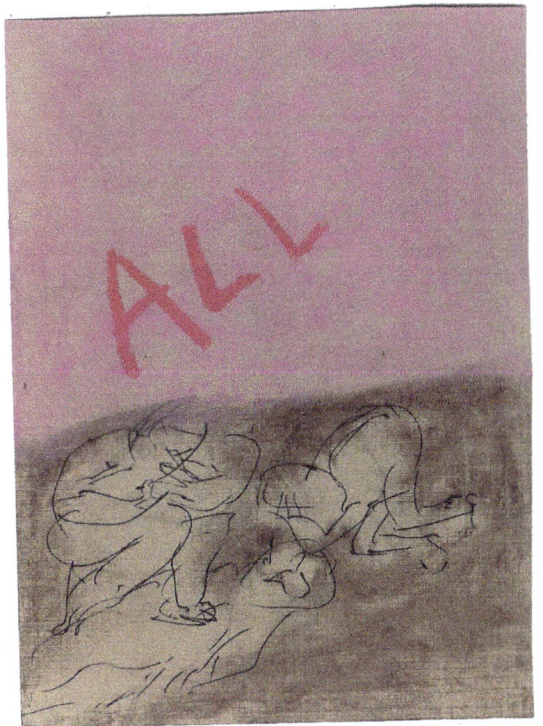

2

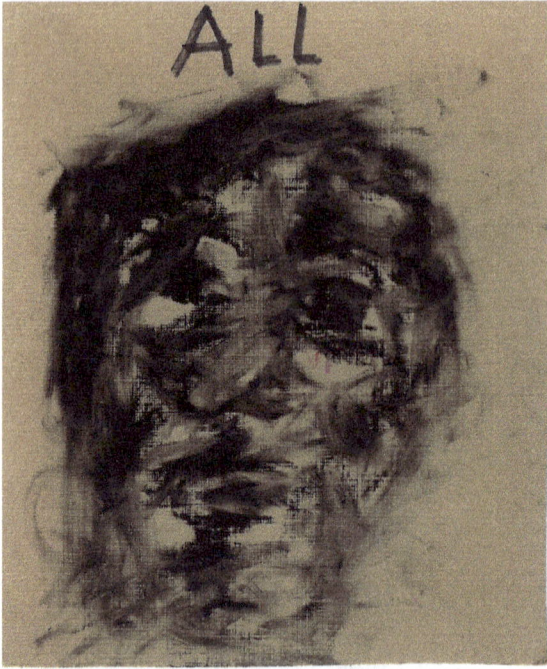

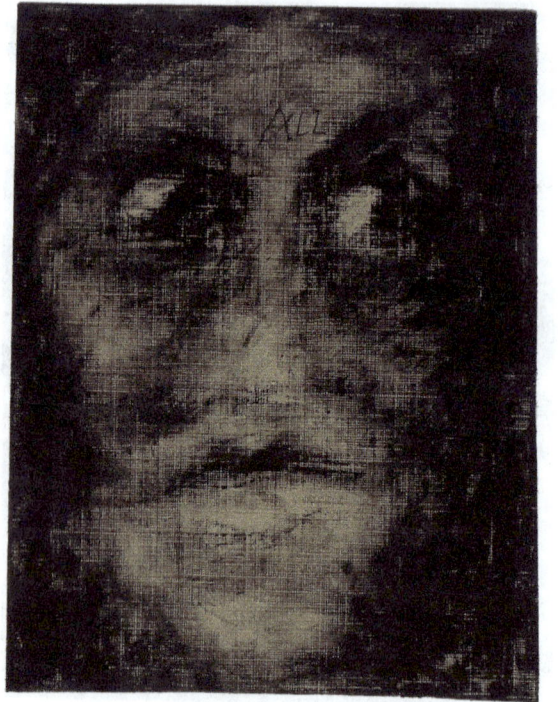

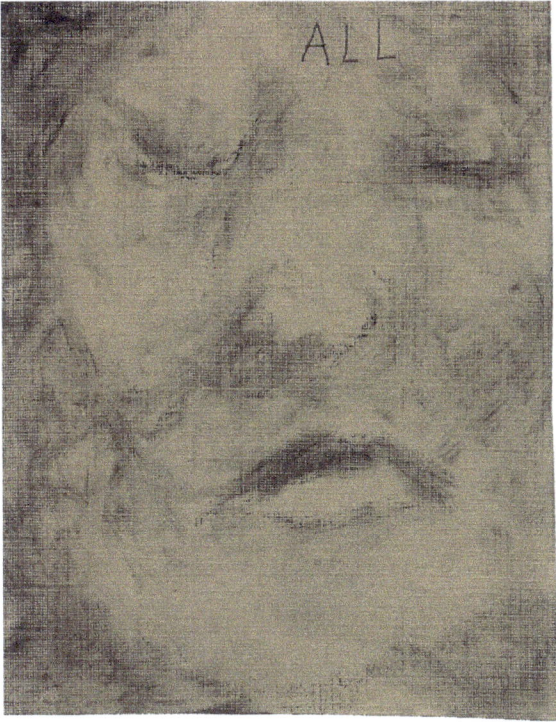

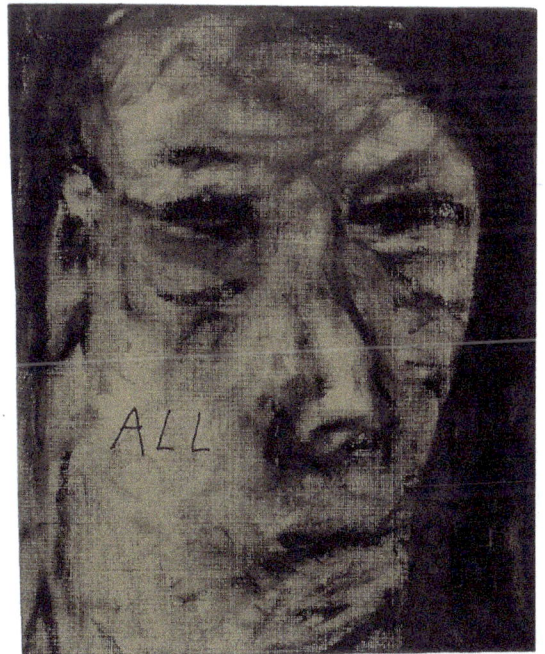

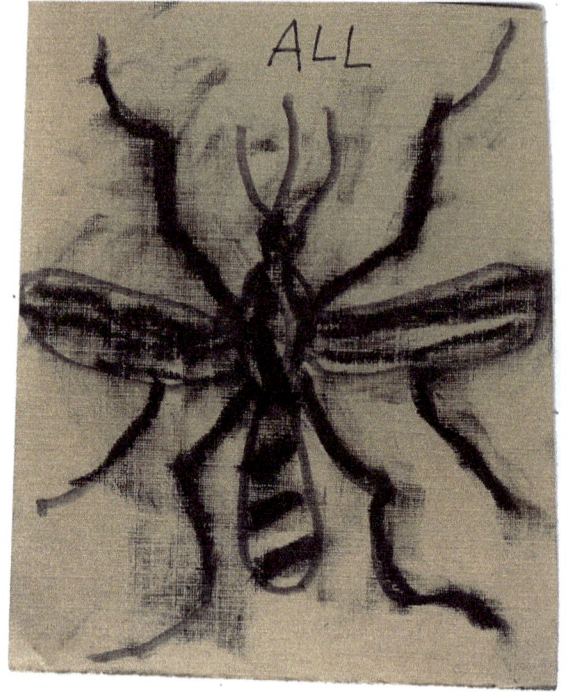

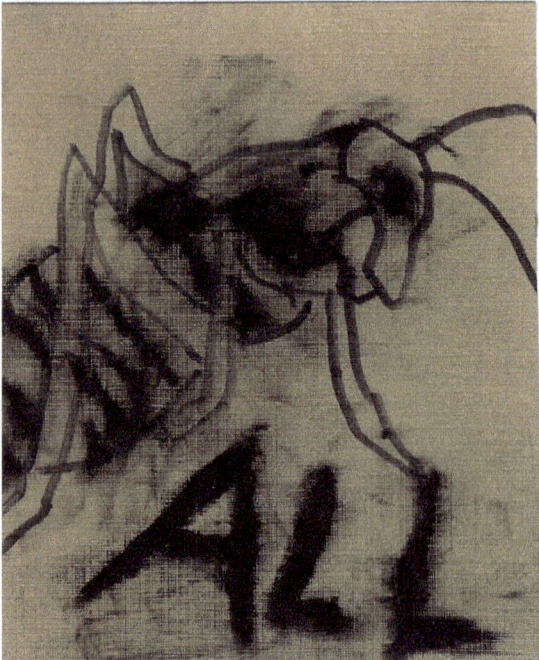

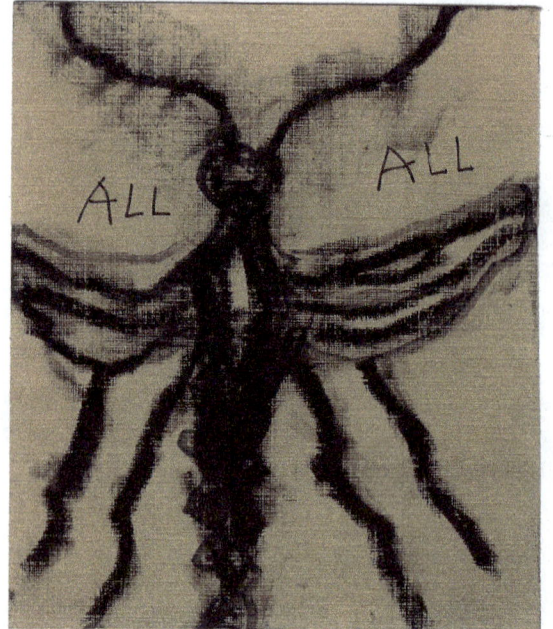

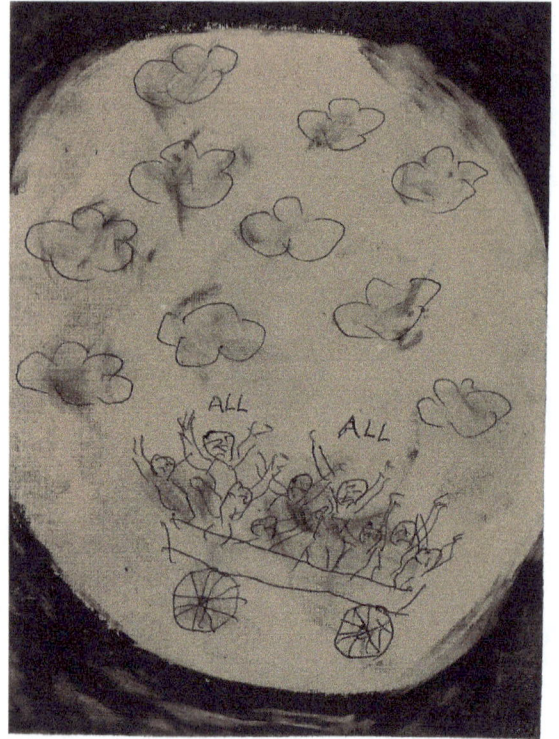

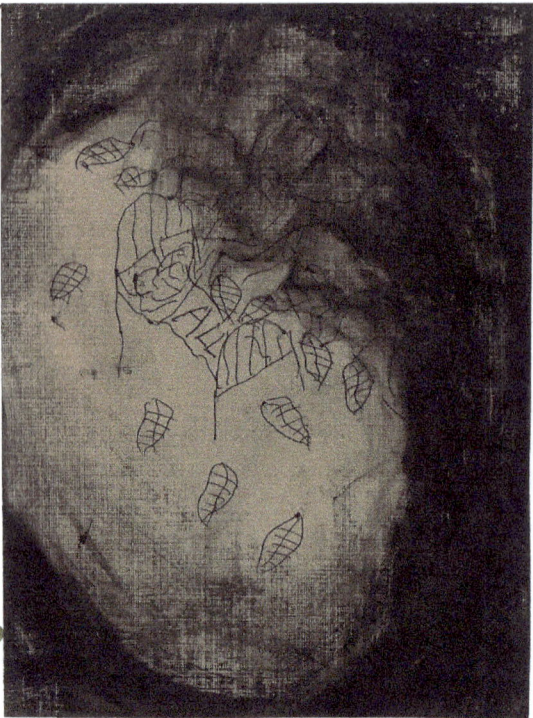

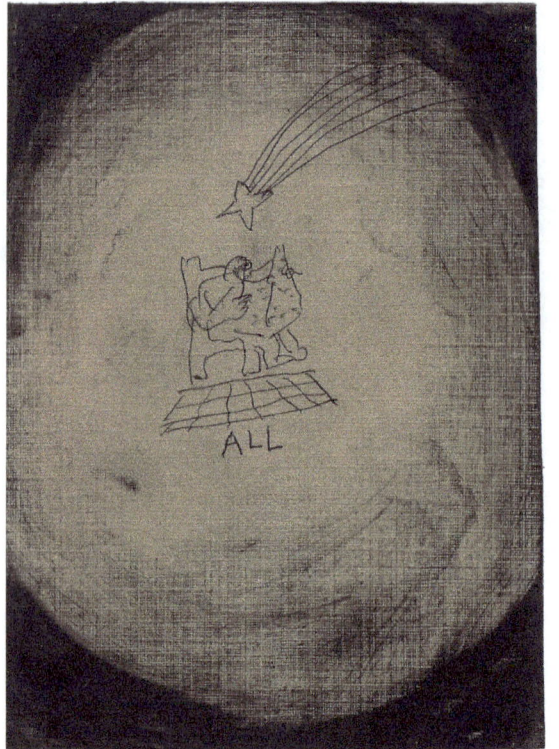

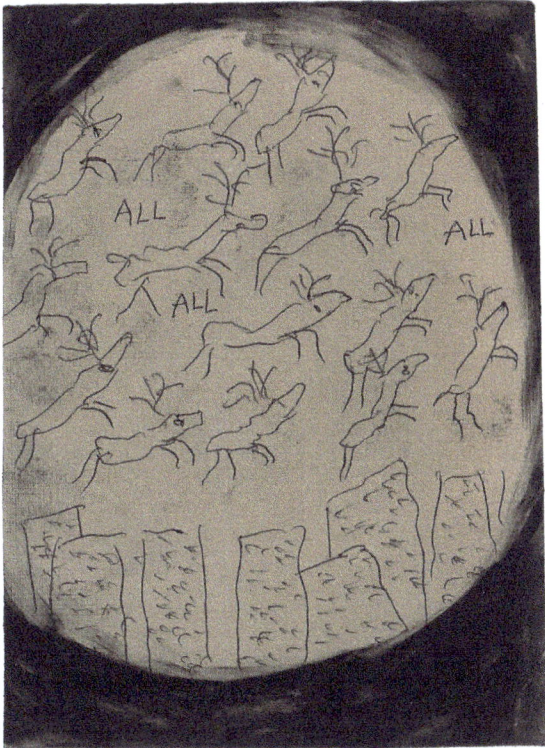

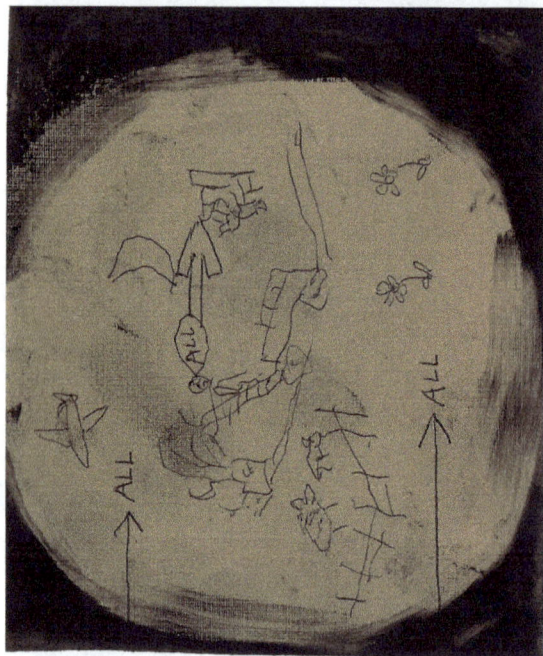

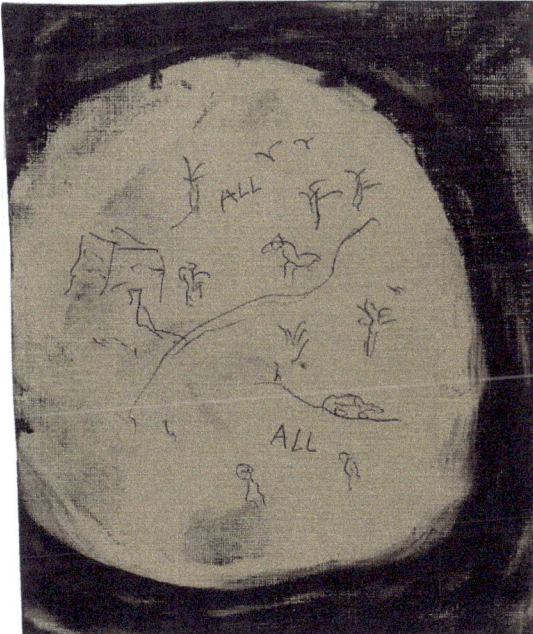

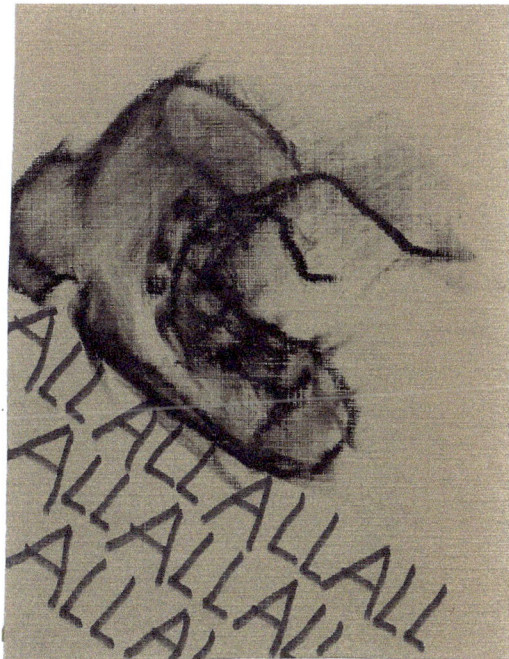

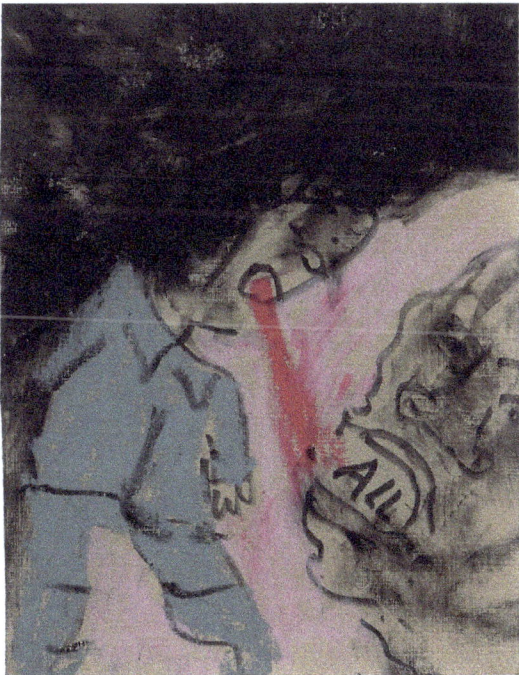
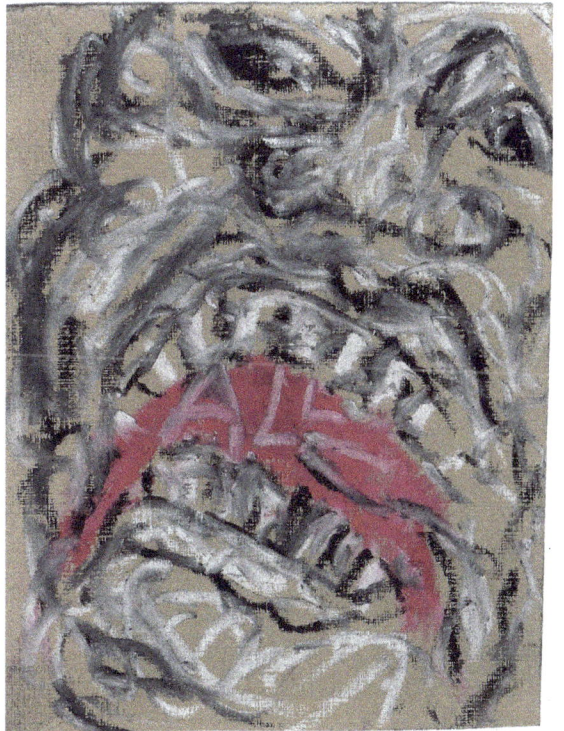

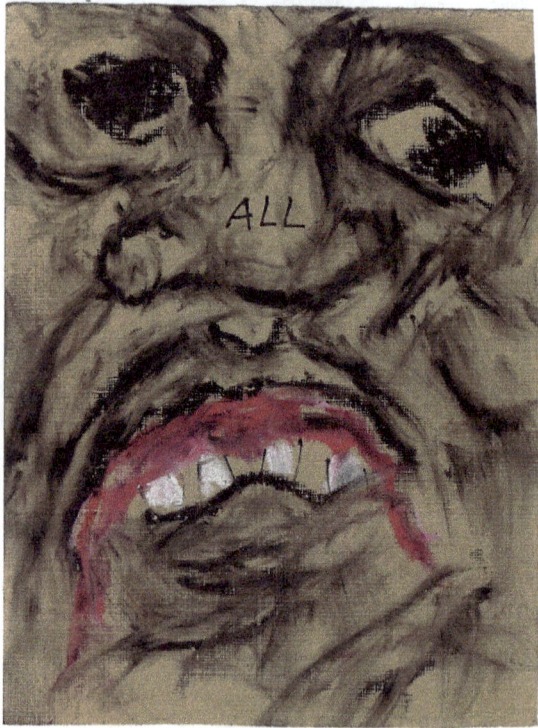

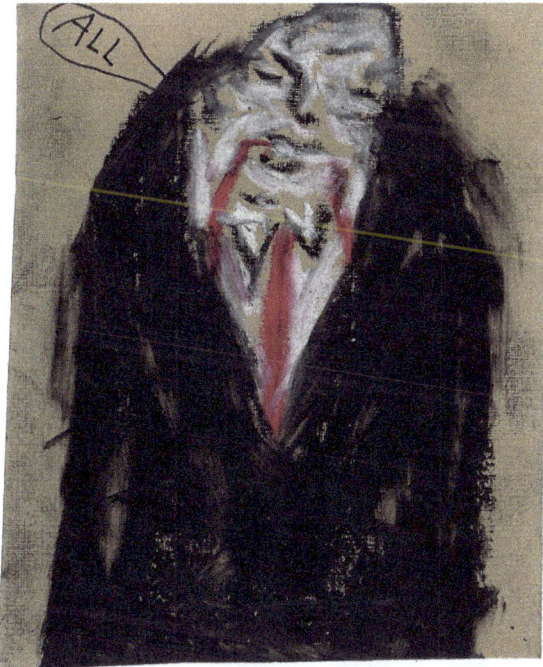

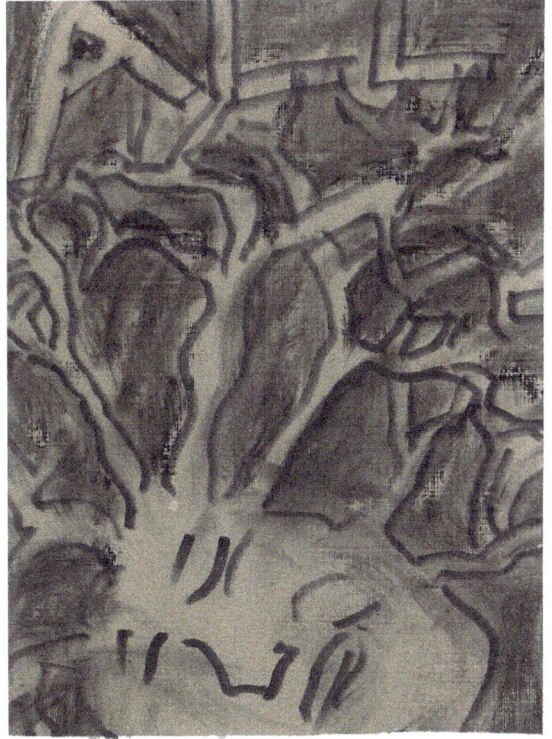

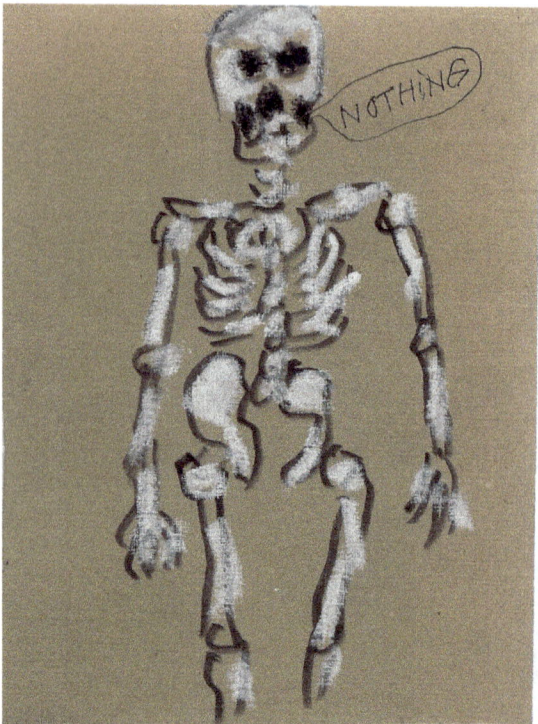

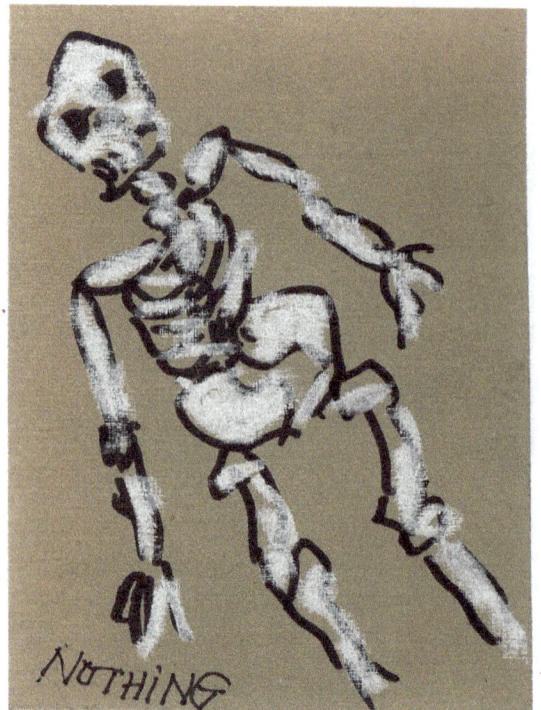

NOTHING

NOTHING

NOTHING

NOTHING

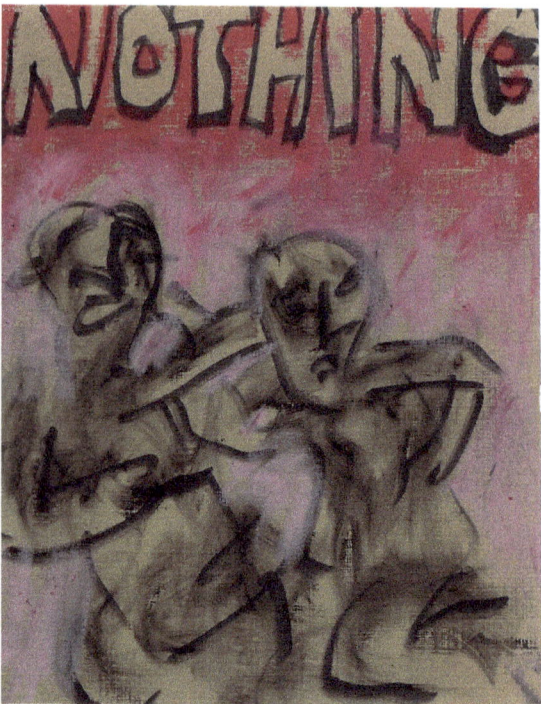

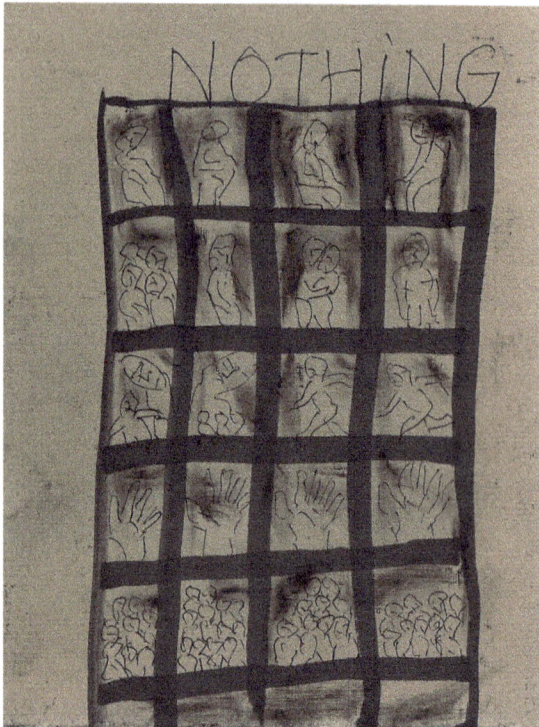

NOTHING

NOTHING

NOTHING

NOTHING

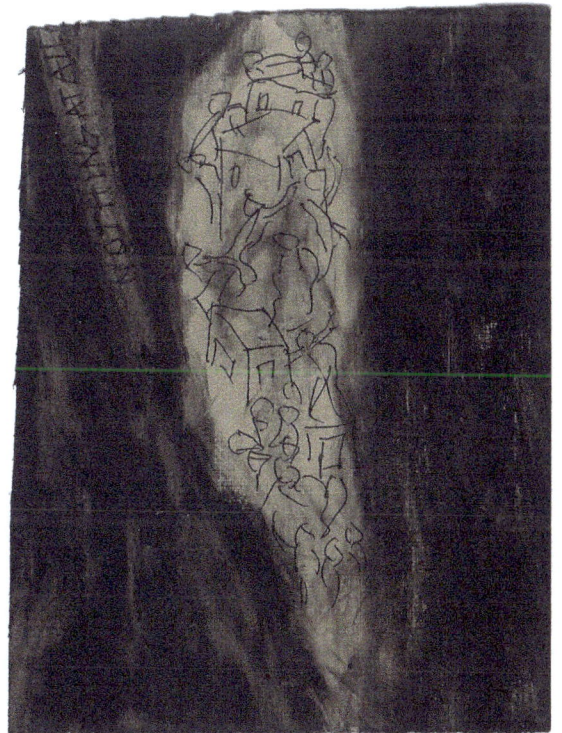

44

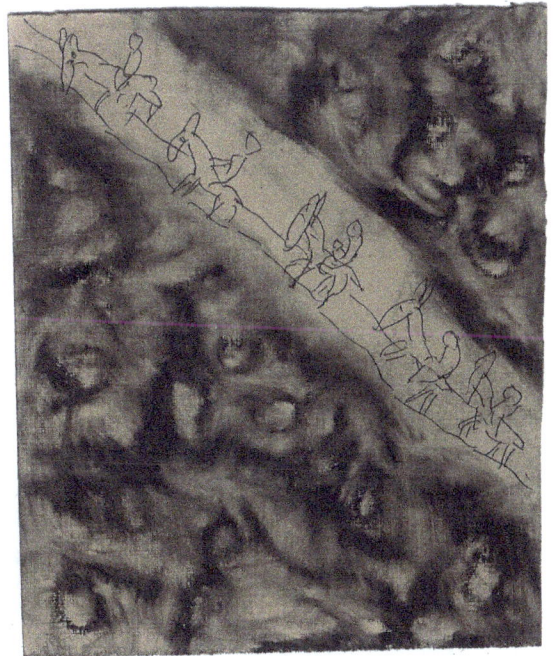

47

Fomite
58 Peru Street
Burlington, VT 05401
This book was collectively designed Donna Bister, Marc Estrin & Peter Schumann

Peter Schumann is the founder and director of the Bread & Puppet Theater. Born in Silesia, he was a sculptor and dancer in Germany before moving to the United States in 1961.

Other Peter Schumann books
from Fomite

All

All, Nothing, Nothing At All

We

Faust 3

Bread & Sentences

Life and Death of Charlotte Salomon

Planet Kasper Volumes One and Two

Diagonal Man Volumes One and Two

Belligerent & Not So Belligerent Slogans
from the Possibilitarian Arsenal